Sarah Daniel

AIR FRYER CAKES & BAKES VOL. 1

Sweet, mouthwatering treats for the family!

Kensington Recipe Press

© 2021 Kensington Recipe Press - All rights reserved.

Photography Humbert Castillo
Graphic design Yuka Okuma
Editorial coordination Lizzie Martin

First edition March 2021

The following book is reproduced below to provide information that is as accurate and reliable as possible. Regardless, purchasing this book can be seen as consent because both the publisher and the author of this book are in no way experts on the topics discussed within. Any recommendations or suggestions that are made herein are for entertainment purposes only. Professionals should be consulted as needed before undertaking any of the actions endorsed herein. This declaration is deemed fair and valid by both the American Bar Association and the Committee of Publishers Association and is legally binding throughout the United States. Furthermore, the transmission, duplication, or reproduction of any of the following work, including specific information, will be considered an illegal act irrespective of if it is done electronically or in print. This extends to creating a secondary or tertiary copy of the work or a recorded document and can only express written consent from the publisher. All additional rights reserved. The information in the following pages is broadly considered a truthful and accurate account of facts. As such, any inattention, use, or misuse of the information in question by the reader will render any resulting actions solely under their purview. There are no scenarios in which the publisher or the original author of this work can be in any fashion deemed liable for any hardship or damages that may befall them after undertaking the information described herein. Additionally, the following pages' information is intended only for informational purposes and should thus be thought of as universal. As befitting its nature, it is presented without assurance regarding its prolonged validity or interim quality. Trademarks that are mentioned are done without written consent and can in no way be considered an endorsement from the trademark holder.

Table of Content

INTRODUCTION	6
CAKES & BAKES	8
Raspberry Pudding Surprise	9
Double Chocolate Cake	11
Homemade Coconut Banana Treat	13
Banana Oatmeal Cookies	15
Chocolate Lava Cake	17
Chocolate Molten Lava Cake	19
Sweet & Crisp Bananas	21
Shortbread Fingers	23
Pear & Apple Crisp with Walnuts	25
Roasted Pumpkin Seeds & Cinnamon	27
Fried Pineapple Rings	29
Swedish Chocolate Mug Cake	31
Chocolate Cookies	33
Pumpkin Cinnamon Pudding	35
Poppy Seed Pound Cake	37
Apple Wedges	39
Sugar Butter Fritters	41
Dunky Dough Dippers & Chocolate Sauce	43
Cheesy Lemon Cake	45
Peach Slices	47
Mixed Berry Puffed Pastry	49
New England Pumpkin Cake	51
Glazed Donuts	53
Lusciously Easy Brownies	55
Avocado Pudding	57
Sponge Cake	59
Peach Crumble	61
Coffee Surprise	63
Vanilla Souffle	65
Raspberry Muffins	67
Pecan Pie	69
Peanut Butter Cookies	71
Blackberry Crisp	73
Melts in Your Mouth Caramel Cheesecake	75
Butter Marshmallow Fluff Turnover	77
Orange Carrot Cake	79
English Lemon Tarts	81

Keto-Friendly Doughnut Recipe	83
Maple Cinnamon Buns	85
Cherry Pie	87
Apple Pie	89
Oriental Coconut Cake	91
Pound Cake with Fresh Apples	93
Raspberry-Coco Dessert	95
Lava Cake in A Mug	97
Blueberry Pancakes	99
Chocolate Brownies & Caramel Sauce	101

Introduction

Sarah Daniel is a passionate cookbook writer with over two decades of professional culinary expertise. Known for her culinary skills and high standard, she has combined her classic recipes tailored to use with the modern cooking appliance in her new cookbook series "The Complete Air Fryer Cookbook" for Kensington Recipe Press. She loves to employ innovations in cooking by keeping the traditional elements and richness.

We can always find the art of simplicity in her recipes, making her a step ahead of many innovative cooking methods. All of her books include self-tested recipes, and the pleasure of sharing exciting experiments is evident in most of her recipe works.

Popularly known as a "recipe development whiz" among her circle, she contributes recipes to several reputed magazines. She helps you discover something new and impressive. Beyond her books, she maintains a strong influence among her friends and family as an enthusiast of healthy eating and living.

Having spent considerable time writing the series "The Complete Air Fryer Cookbook", Sarah has carefully penned her research with super versatile meal ideas without compromising quality and nutritional values. Her approach to modern food tech is mind-blowing.

This Cookbook Series is a pioneering endeavor blended with modern cooking with traditional values by focusing on healthy, balanced food. It is a reference series for people who love having healthy food.

Cakes & Bakes

Raspberry Pudding Surprise

Ready about in: 40 min | Servings: 1 | Easy

Ingredients

3 tablespoons chia seeds

½ cup unsweetened milk

1 scoop chocolate protein powder

¼ cup raspberries, fresh or frozen

1 teaspoon honey

Direction:

Combine the milk, protein powder and chia seeds together.

Let rest for 5 minutes before stirring.

Refrigerate for 30 minutes.

Top with raspberries.

Serve and Enjoy!

Double Chocolate Cake

Ready about in: 45 min | Servings: 8 | Easy

Ingredients

½ cup sugar

1 ¼ cups flour

1 teaspoon baking powder

⅓ cup cocoa powder

¼ teaspoon ground cloves

1/8 teaspoon freshly grated nutmeg

Pinch of table salt

1 egg

¼ cup soda of your choice

¼ cup milk

½ stick butter, melted

2 ounce bittersweet chocolate, melted

½ cup hot water

Direction:

In a bowl, thoroughly combine the dry ingredients.

In another bowl, mix together the egg, soda, milk, butter, and chocolate.

Combine the two mixtures. Add in the water and stir well.

Take a cake pan that is small enough to fit inside your Air Fryer and transfer the mixture to the pan.

Place a sheet of foil on top and bake at 320° F for 35 minutes.

Take off the foil and bake for further 10 minutes.

Frost the cake with buttercream if desired before serving.

Homemade Coconut Banana Treat

Ready about in: 20 min | Servings: 6 | Easy

Ingredients

2 tablespoons coconut oil

¾ cup friendly bread crumbs

2 tablespoons sugar

½ teaspoon cinnamon powder

¼ teaspoon ground cloves

6 ripe bananas, peeled and halved

⅓ cup flour

1 large egg, beaten

Direction:

Heat a skillet over a medium heat. Add in the coconut oil and the bread crumbs, and mix together for approximately 4 minutes.

Take the skillet off of the heat.

Add in the sugar, cinnamon, and cloves.

Cover all sides of the banana halves with the rice flour.

Dip each one in the beaten egg before coating them in the bread crumb mix.

Place the banana halves in the Air Fryer basket, taking care not to overlap them. Cook at 290° F for 10 minutes. You may need to complete this step in multiple batches.

Serve hot or at room temperature, topped with a sprinkling of flaked coconut if desired.

Banana Oatmeal Cookies

Ready about in: 20 min | Servings: 6 | Easy

Ingredients

2 cups quick oats

¼ cup milk

4 ripe bananas, mashed

¼ cup coconut, shredded

Direction:

Select bake mode the set the temperature to pre-heat the Air Fryer to 350° F.

Combine all of the ingredients in a bowl.

Scoop equal amounts of the cookie dough onto a baking sheet and put it in the Air Fryer basket.

Bake the cookies for 15 minutes.

When the timer reaches 0, then press the cancel button

Serve and Enjoy!

Chocolate Lava Cake

Ready about in: 20 min | Servings: 4 | Easy

Ingredients

1 cup dark cocoa candy melts

1 stick butter

2 eggs

4 tablespoons sugar

1 tablespoons honey

4 tablespoons flour

Pinch of kosher salt

Pinch of ground cloves

¼ teaspoon grated nutmeg

¼ teaspoon cinnamon powder

Direction:

Spritz the insides of four custard cups with cooking spray.

Melt the cocoa candy melts and butter in the microwave for 30 seconds to 1 minute.

In a large bowl, combine the eggs, sugar and honey with a whisk until frothy. Pour in the melted chocolate mix.

Throw in the rest of the ingredients and combine well with an electric mixer or a manual whisk.

Transfer equal portions of the mixture into the prepared custard cups.

Place in the Air Fryer and air bake at 350° F for 12 minutes.

Remove from the Air Fryer and allow to cool for 5 to 6 minutes.

Place each cup upside-down on a dessert plate and let the cake slide out. Serve with fruits and chocolate syrup if desired.

Chocolate Molten Lava Cake

Ready about in: 25 min | Servings: 4 | Easy

Ingredients

3 ½ ounce butter, melted

3 ½ tablespoons sugar

3 ½ ounce chocolate, melted

1 ½ tablespoons flour

2 eggs

Direction:

Select bake mode the set the temperature to pre-heat the Air Fryer to 375° F.

Grease four ramekins with a little butter.

Rigorously combine the eggs and butter before stirring in the melted chocolate.

Slowly fold in the flour.

Spoon an equal amount of the mixture into each ramekin.

Put them in the Air Fryer and cook for 10 minutes

Place the ramekins upside-down on plates and let the cakes fall out. Serve hot.

Sweet & Crisp Bananas

Ready about in: 20 min | Servings: 4 | Easy

Ingredients

4 ripe bananas, peeled and halved

1 tablespoons meal

1 tablespoons cashew, crushed

1 egg, beaten

1 ½ tablespoons coconut oil

¼ cup flour

1 ½ tablespoons sugar

½ cup friendly bread crumbs

Direction:

Put the coconut oil in a saucepan and heat over a medium heat. Stir in the bread crumbs and cook, stirring continuously, for 4 minutes. Transfer the bread crumbs to a bowl.

Add in the meal and crushed cashew. Mix well.

Coat each of the banana halves in the corn flour, before dipping it in the beaten egg and lastly coating it with the bread crumbs.

Put the coated banana halves in the Air Fryer basket. Season with the sugar.

Air Fry at 350°F for 10 minutes.

When the timer reaches 0, then press the cancel button

Serve and Enjoy!

Shortbread Fingers

Ready about in: 20 min | Servings: 10 | Easy

Ingredients

1 ½ cups quality unsalted butter

1 cup flour

¾ cup caster sugar

½ teaspoon salt

Homemade Candied Citrus Peel

Cooking spray

Direction:

Select bake mode the set the temperature to pre-heat your Air Fryer to 350° F.

In a bowl. combine the flour and sugar.

Cut each stick of butter into small chunks. Add the chunks into the flour and the sugar.

Blend the butter into the mixture to combine everything well.

Use your hands to knead the mixture, forming a smooth consistency.

Shape the mixture into 10 equal-sized finger shapes, marking them with the tines of a fork for decoration if desired.

Lightly spritz the Air Fryer basket with the cooking spray. Place the cookies inside, spacing them out well.

Bake the cookies for 12 minutes.

Let cool slightly before serving. Alternatively, you can store the cookies in an airtight container for up to 3 days.

Serve and Enjoy!

Pear & Apple Crisp with Walnuts

Ready about in: 25 min | Servings: 6 | Easy

Ingredients

½ lb. apples, cored and chopped

½ lb. pears, cored and chopped

1 cup flour

1 cup sugar

1 tablespoons butter

1 teaspoon ground cinnamon

¼ teaspoon ground cloves

1 teaspoon vanilla extract

¼ cup chopped walnuts

Whipped cream, to serve

Direction:

Lightly grease a baking dish and place the apples and pears inside.

Combine the rest of the ingredients, minus the walnuts and the whipped cream, until a coarse, crumbly texture is achieved.

Pour the mixture over the fruits and spread it evenly. Top with the chopped walnuts.

Air bake at 340°F for 20 minutes or until the top turns golden brown. When cooked through, serve at room temperature with whipped cream.

Roasted Pumpkin Seeds & Cinnamon

Reasy about in: 35 min | Servings: 2 | Easy

Ingredients

1 cup pumpkin raw seeds

1 tablespoons ground cinnamon

2 tablespoons sugar

1 cup water

1 tbsp. olive oil

Direction:

In a frying pan, combine the pumpkin seeds, cinnamon and water.

Boil the mixture over a high heat for 2 - 3 minutes.

Pour out the water and place the seeds on a clean kitchen towel, allowing them to dry for 20 - 30 minutes.

In a bowl, mix together the sugar, dried seeds, a pinch of cinnamon and one tablespoon of olive oil.

Select bake mode the set the temperature to pre-heat the Air Fryer to 340° F.

Place the seed mixture in the Fryer basket and allow to cook for 15 minutes, shaking the basket periodically throughout.

Serve and Enjoy!

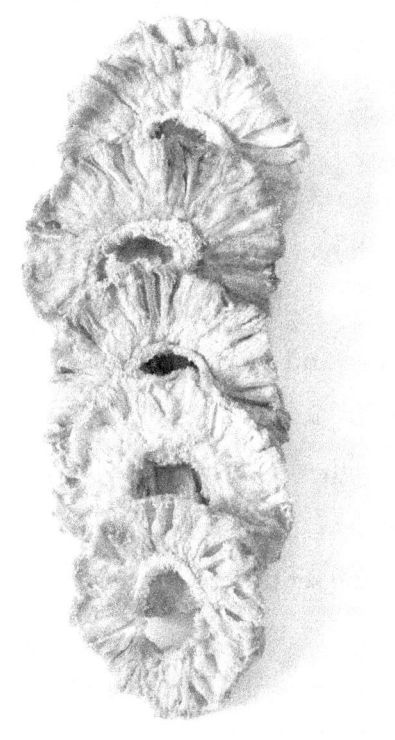

Fried Pineapple Rings

Ready about in: 10 min | Servings: 6 | Normal

Ingredients

2/3 cup flour

½ teaspoon baking powder

½ teaspoon baking soda

Pinch of kosher salt

½ cup water

1 cup rice milk

½ teaspoon ground cinnamon

¼ teaspoon ground anise star

½ teaspoon vanilla essence

1 tablespoons sugar

¼ cup unsweetened flaked coconut

1 medium pineapple, peeled and sliced

Direction:

Mix together all of the ingredients, minus the pineapple.

Cover the pineapple slices with the batter.

Place the slices in the Air Fryer and cook at 380°F for 6 - 8 minutes.

Pour a drizzling of maple syrup over the pineapple and serve with a side of vanilla ice cream.

Swedish Chocolate Mug Cake

Prep + Cook Time: 15 minutes | Servings: 1

Ingredients

1 tablespoons cocoa powder

3 tablespoons coconut oil

¼ cup flour

3 tablespoons whole milk

1 tablespoons sugar

Direction:

In a bowl, stir together all of the ingredients to combine them completely.

Take a short, stout mug and pour the mixture into it.

Put the mug in your Air Fryer and cook for 10 minutes at 390° F.

When the timer reaches 0, then press the cancel button

Serve and Enjoy!

Chocolate Cookies

Ready about in: 30 min | Servings: 8 | Easy

Ingredients

3 ounce sugar

4 ounce butter

1 tablespoons honey

6 ounce flour

1 ½ tablespoons milk

2 ounce chocolate chips

Direction:

Select bake mode the set the temperature to pre-heat the Air Fryer to 350° F.

Mix together the sugar and butter using an electric mixer, until a fluffy texture is achieved.

Stir in the remaining ingredients, minus the chocolate chips.

Gradually fold in the chocolate chips.

Spoon equal portions of the mixture onto a lined baking sheet and flatten out each one with a spoon. Ensure the cookies are not touching.

Place in the Fryer and cook for 18 minutes.

When the timer reaches 0, then press the cancel button

Serve and Enjoy!

Pumpkin Cinnamon Pudding

Ready about in: 25 minutes | Servings: 4 | Normal

Ingredients

3 cups pumpkin puree

3 tablespoons honey

1 tablespoons ginger

1 tablespoons cinnamon

1 teaspoon clove

1 teaspoon nutmeg

1 cup full-fat cream

2 eggs

1 cup sugar

Direction:

Select bake mode the set the temperature to pre-heat your Air Fryer to 390° F.

In a bowl, stir all of the ingredients together to combine.

Grease the inside of a small baking dish.

Pour the mixture into the dish and transfer to the Fryer. Cook for 15 minutes.

When the timer reaches 0, then press the cancel button

Serve with whipped cream if desired.

Poppy Seed Pound Cake

Ready about in: 20 min | Serves 8 | Normal

Ingredients

¼ cup erythritol powder

¼ teaspoon vanilla extract

½ cup coconut milk

1 ½ cups almond flour

1 ½ teaspoon baking powder

1/3 cup butter, unsalted

2 large eggs, beaten

2 tablespoon psyllium husk powder

2 tablespoons poppy seeds

Direction:

Select bake mode the set the temperature to preheat the Air Fryer for 5 minutes.

In a mixing bowl, combine all ingredients.

Use a hand mixer to mix everything.

Pour into a small loaf pan that will fit in the Air Fryer.

Bake for 20 minutes at 375° F or until a toothpick inserted in the middle comes out clean.

Serve and Enjoy!

Apple Wedges

Ready about in: 25 min | Servings: 4 | Easy

Ingredients

4 large apples

2 tablespoon olive oil

½ cup dried apricots, chopped

1 – 2 tablespoon sugar

½ teaspoon ground cinnamon

Direction:

Peel the apples and slice them into eight wedges. Throw away the cores. Coat the apple wedges with the oil.

Place each wedge in the Air Fryer and cook for 12 - 15 minutes at 350°F.

Add in the apricots and allow to cook for a further 3 minutes.

Stir together the sugar and cinnamon. Sprinkle this mixture over the cooked apples before serving.

Sugar Butter Fritters

Ready about in: 30 min | Servings: 16 | Easy

Ingredients

For the dough:

4 cups flour

1 teaspoon kosher salt

1 teaspoon sugar

3 tablespoon butter, at room temperature

1 packet instant yeast

1 ¼ cups lukewarm water

For the Cakes

1 cup sugar

Pinch of cardamom

1 teaspoon cinnamon powder

1 stick butter, melted

Direction:

Place all of the ingredients in a large bowl and combine well.

Add in the lukewarm water and mix until a soft, elastic dough forms. Place the dough on a lightly floured surface and lay a greased sheet of aluminum foil on top of the dough. Refrigerate for 5 to 10 minutes. Remove it from the refrigerator and divide it in two. Mold each half into a log and slice it into 20 pieces.

In a shallow bowl, combine the sugar, cardamom and cinnamon. Coat the slices with a light brushing of melted butter and the sugar. Spritz Air Fryer basket with cooking spray.

Transfer the slices to the Fryer and Air Fry at 360° F for roughly 10 minutes. Turn each slice once during the baking time.
Dust each slice with the sugar before serving.

Dunky Dough Dippers & Chocolate Sauce

Ready about in: 45 min | Servings: 5 | Normal

Ingredients

¾ cup sugar

1 lb. friendly bread dough

1 cup heavy cream

12 ounce high quality semi-sweet chocolate chips

½ cup butter, melted

2 tablespoon extract

Direction:

Select bake mode the set the temperature to pre-heat the Air Fryer to 350° F.

Coat the inside of the basket with a little melted butter.

Halve and roll up the dough to create 2 15-inch logs. Slice each log into 20 disks.

Halve each disk and twist it 3 or 4 times.

Lay out a cookie sheet and lay the twisted dough pieces on top. Brush the pieces with some more melted butter and sprinkle on the sugar.

Place the sheet in the Air Fryer and air fry for 5 minutes. Flip the dough twists over, and brush the other side with more butter. Cook for an additional 3 minutes. It may be necessary to complete this step in batches.

In the meantime, make the chocolate sauce. Firstly, put the heavy cream into a saucepan over the medium heat and allow it to simmer.

Put the chocolate chips into a large bowl and add the simmering cream on top. Whisk the chocolate chips everything together until a smooth consistency is achieved. Stir in 2 tablespoons of extract.

Transfer the baked cookies in a shallow dish, pour over the rest of the melted butter and sprinkle on the sugar.

Drizzle on the chocolate sauce before serving.

Cheesy Lemon Cake

Ready about in: 60 minutes | Servings: 6 | Normal

Ingredients

17.5 ounce ricotta cheese

5.4 ounce sugar

3 eggs

3 tablespoon flour

1 lemon, juiced and zested

2 teaspoon vanilla extract [optional]

Direction:

Select bake mode the set the temperature to pre-heat Air Fryer to 320°F.

Combine all of the ingredients until a creamy consistency is achieved.

Place the mixture in a cake tin.

Transfer the tin to the Fryer and cook the cakes for 25 minutes.

Remove the cake from the Fryer, allow to cool, and serve.

Peach Slices

Ready about in: 40 minutes | Servings: 4 | Easy

Ingredients

4 cups peaches, sliced

2 - 3 tablespoon sugar

2 tablespoon flour

⅓ cup oats

2 tablespoon unsalted butter

¼ teaspoon vanilla extract

1 teaspoon cinnamon

Direction:

In a large bowl, combine the peach slices, sugar, vanilla extract, and cinnamon. Pour the mixture into a baking tin and place it in the Air Fryer.

Cook for 20 minutes on 290° F.

In the meantime, combine the oats, flour, and unsalted butter in a separate bowl.

Once the peach slices cooked, pour the butter mixture on top of them.

Cook for an additional 10 minutes at 300 - 310° F.

Remove from the fryer and allow to crisp up for 5 - 10.

Serve with ice cream if desired.

Mixed Berry Puffed Pastry

Ready about in: 20 min | Servings: 3 | Normal

Ingredients

3 pastry dough sheets

½ cup mixed berries, mashed

1 tablespoon honey

2 tablespoon cream cheese

3 tablespoon chopped walnuts

¼ teaspoon vanilla extract

Direction:

Select bake mode the set the temperature to pre-heat your Air Fryer to 375° F.

Roll out the pastry sheets and spread the cream cheese over each one.

In a bowl, combine the berries, vanilla extract and honey.

Cover a baking sheet with parchment paper.

Spoon equal amounts of the berry mixture into the center of each sheet of pastry. Scatter the chopped walnuts on top.

Fold up the pastry around the filling and press down the edges with the back of a fork to seal them.

Transfer the baking sheet to the Air Fryer and cook for approximately 15 minutes.

When the timer reaches 0, then press the cancel button

Serve and Enjoy

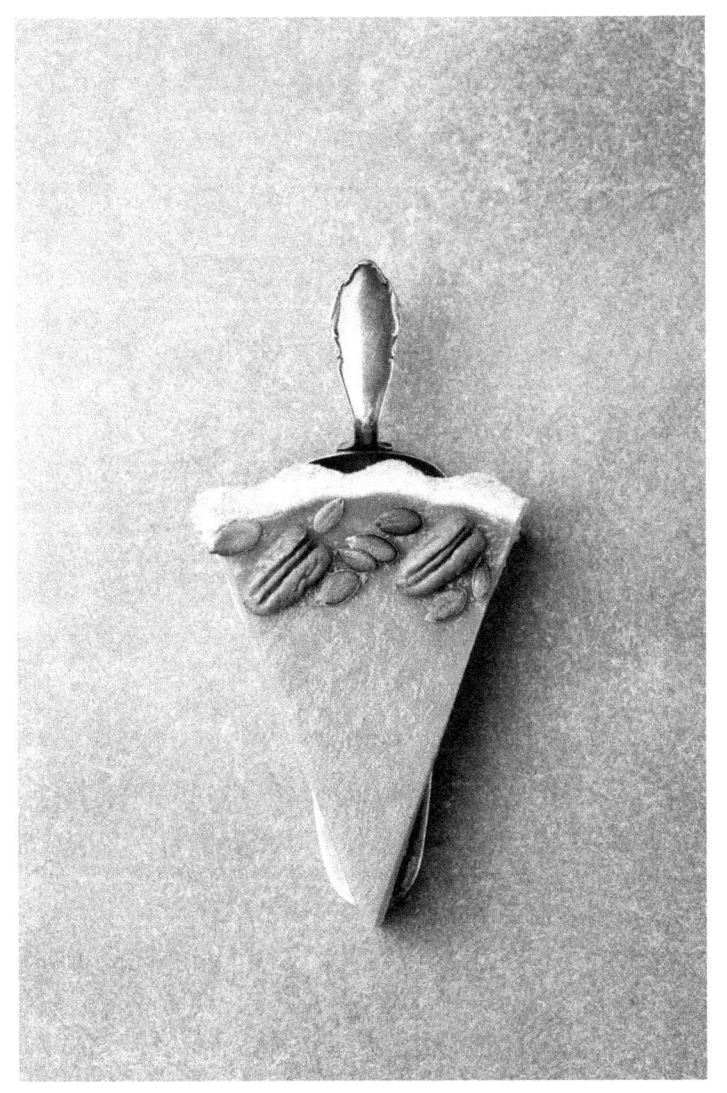

New England Pumpkin Cake

Ready about in: 50 min | Servings: 4 | Normal

Ingredients

1 large egg

½ cup skimmed milk

7 ounce flour

2 tablespoon sugar

5 ounce pumpkin puree

Pinch of salt

Pinch of cinnamon [if desired]

Cooking spray

Direction:

Stir together the pumpkin puree and sugar in a bowl. Crack in the egg and combine using a whisk until smooth.

Add in the flour and salt, stirring constantly. Pour in the milk, ensuring to combine everything well.

Spritz a baking tin with cooking spray.

Transfer the batter to the baking tin.

Select bake mode the set the temperature to pre-heat the Air Fryer to 350° F.

Put the tin in the Air Fryer basket and bake for 15 minutes.

When the timer reaches 0, then press the cancel button

Serve and Enjoy!

Glazed Donuts

Ready about in: 25 minutes | Servings: 2 – 4 | Easy

Ingredients

1 can [8 ounce] refrigerated croissant dough

Cooking spray

1 can [16 ounce] vanilla frosting

Direction:

Cut the croissant dough into 1-inch-round slices. Make a hole in the center of each one to create a donut.

Put the donuts in the Air Fryer basket, taking care not to overlap any, and spritz with cooking spray. You may need to cook everything in multiple batches.

Cook at 400° F for 2 minutes. Turn the donuts over and cook for another 3 minutes.

Place the rolls on a paper plate.

Microwave a half-cup of frosting for 30 seconds and pour a drizzling of the frosting over the donuts before serving.

Lusciously Easy Brownies

Ready about in: 20 min | Serves 8 | Easy

Ingredients

1 egg

2 tablespoons and 2 teaspoons unsweetened cocoa powder

1/2 cup white sugar

1/2 teaspoon vanilla extract

1/4 cup butter

1/4 cup all-purpose flour

1/8 teaspoon salt

1/8 teaspoon baking powder

Frosting:

1 tablespoon and 1-1/2 teaspoons butter, softened

1 tablespoon and 1-1/2 teaspoons unsweetened cocoa powder

1-1/2 teaspoons honey

1/2 teaspoon vanilla extract

1/2 cup confectioners' sugar

Direction:

Lightly grease baking pan of Air Fryer with cooking spray. Melt ¼ cup butter for 3 minutes. Stir in vanilla, eggs, and sugar. Mix well. Stir in baking powder, salt, flour, and cocoa mix well. Evenly spread. For 20 minutes, cook on 300° F.

In a small bowl, make the frosting by mixing well all Ingredients. Frost brownies while still warm.

Serve and enjoy.

Avocado Pudding

Ready about in: 5 minutes | Servings: 1

Ingredients

Avocado

3 teaspoon liquid Sugar

1 tablespoon cocoa powder

4 teaspoon unsweetened milk

¼ teaspoon vanilla extract

Direction:

Select bake mode the set the temperature to pre-heat your Air Fryer at 360° F.

Halve the avocado, twist to open, and scoop out the pit.

Spoon the flesh into a bowl and mash it with a fork. Throw in the Sugar, cocoa powder, milk, and vanilla extract, and combine everything with a hand mixer.

Transfer this mixture to the basket of your Fryer and cook for 3 minutes.

When the timer reaches 0, then press the cancel button

Serve and Enjoy!

Sponge Cake

Prep + Cook Time: 50 minutes | Servings: 8

Ingredients

For the Cake:

9 ounce sugar

9 ounce butter

3 eggs

9 ounce flour

1 teaspoon vanilla extract

Zest of 1 lemon

1 tsp. baking powder

For the Frosting

Juice of 1 lemon

Zest of 1 lemon

1 teaspoon yellow food coloring

7 ounce sugar

4 egg whites

Direction:

Select bake mode the set the temperature to pre-heat your Air Fryer to 320° F.

Use an electric mixer to combine all of the cake ingredients.

Grease the insides of two round cake pans.

Pour an equal amount of the batter into each pan.

Place one pan in the Fryer and cook for 15 minutes, before repeating with the second pan.

In the meantime, mix together all of the frosting ingredients.

Allow the cakes to cool. Spread the frosting on top of one cake and stack the other cake on top.

Peach Crumble

Ready about in: 35 min | Servings: 6 | Easy

Ingredients

1 ½ lb. peaches, peeled and chopped

2 tablespoon lemon juice

1 cup flour

1 tablespoon water

½ cup sugar

5 tablespoon cold butter

Pinch of sea salt

Direction:

Mash the peaches a little with a fork to achieve a lumpy consistency. Add in two tablespoons of sugar and the lemon juice.

In a bowl, combine the flour, salt, and sugar. Throw in a tablespoon of water before adding in the cold butter, mixing until crumbly.

Grease the inside of a baking dish and arrange the berries at the bottom. Top with the crumbs.

Transfer the dish to the Air Fryer and air fry for 20 minutes at 390° F. When the timer reaches 0, then press the cancel button

Serve and Enjoy!

Coffee Surprise

Ready about in: 5 minutes | Servings: 1 | Easy

Ingredients

2 heaped tbsp flaxseed, ground

100 ml cooking cream 35% fat

½ teaspoon cocoa powder, dark and unsweetened

1 tablespoon goji berries

Freshly brewed coffee

Direction:

Mix together the flaxseeds, cream and cocoa and coffee.

Season with goji berries.

Serve and Enjoy.

Vanilla Souffle

Ready about in: 50 minutes | Servings: 6 | Easy

Ingredients

¼ cup flour

¼ cup butter, softened

1 cup whole milk

¼ cup sugar

2 teaspoon vanilla extract

1 vanilla bean

5 egg whites

4 egg yolks

1 ounce sugar

1 teaspoon cream of tartar

Direction:

Mix together the flour and butter to create a smooth paste.

In a saucepan, heat up the milk. Add the ¼ cup sugar and allow it to dissolve.

Put the vanilla bean in the mixture and bring it to a boil.

Pour in the flour-butter mixture. Beat the contents of the saucepan thoroughly with a wire whisk, removing all the lumps.

Reduce the heat and allow the mixture to simmer and thicken for a number of minutes.

Take the saucepan off the heat. Remove the vanilla bean and let the mixture cool for 10 minutes in an ice bath.

In the meantime, grease size 3-oz. ramekins or soufflé dishes with butter and add a sprinkling of sugar to each one.

In a separate bowl quickly, rigorously stir the egg yolks and vanilla extract together. Combine with the milk mixture.

In another bowl, beat the egg whites, 1 oz. sugar and cream of tartar to form medium stiff peaks. Fold the egg whites into the soufflé base. Transfer everything to the ramekins, smoothing the surfaces with a knife or the back of a spoon.

Select bake mode the set the temperature to pre-heat the Air Fryer to 330° F.

Put the ramekins in the cooking basket and cook for 14 – 16 minutes. You may need to complete this step in multiple batches.

Serve the soufflés topped with powdered sugar and with a side of chocolate sauce.

Raspberry Muffins

Ready about in: 35 min | Servings: 10 | Normal

Ingredients

1 egg

1 cup frozen raspberries, coated with some flour

1 ½ cups flour

½ cup sugar

⅓ cup vegetable oil

2 teaspoon baking powder

Yogurt, as needed

1 teaspoon lemon zest

2 tablespoon lemon juice

Pinch of sea salt

Direction:

Select bake mode the set the temperature to pre-heat the Air Fryer to 350° F

Place all of the dry ingredients in a bowl and combine well.

Beat the egg and pour it into a cup. Mix it with the oil and lemon juice. Add in the yogurt, to taste.

Mix together the dry and wet ingredients.

Add in the lemon zest and raspberries.

Coat the insides of 10 muffin tins with a little butter.

Spoon an equal amount of the mixture into each muffin tin.

Transfer to the Fryer, and cook for 10 minutes, in batches if necessary.

Serve and Enjoy!

Pecan Pie

Ready about in: 1 hour 10 minutes | Servings: 4 | Easy

Ingredients

1x 8-inch pie dough

½ teaspoon cinnamon

¾ teaspoon vanilla extract

2 eggs

¾ cup maple syrup

1/8 teaspoon nutmeg

2 tablespoon butter

1 tablespoon butter, melted

2 tablespoon sugar

½ cup chopped pecans

Direction:

Select bake mode the set the temperature to pre-heat the Air Fryer to 370° F.

In a small bowl, coat the pecans in the melted butter.

Transfer the pecans to the Air Fryer and allow them to toast for about 10 minutes.

Put the pie dough in a greased pie pan and add the pecans on top.

In a bowl, mix together the rest of the ingredients. Pour this over the pecans.

Place the pan in the Fryer and bake for 25 minutes.

When the timer reaches 0, then press the cancel button

Serve and Enjoy

Peanut Butter Cookies

Ready about in: 15 min | Servings: 1 | Easy

Ingredients

¼ teaspoon salt

4 tablespoon erythritol

½ cup peanut butter

1 egg

Direction:

Combine the salt, erythritol, and peanut butter in a bowl, incorporating everything well. Break the egg over the mixture and mix to create a dough.

Flatten the dough using a rolling pin and cut into shapes with a knife or cookie cutter. Make a crisscross on the top of each cookie with a fork.

Select bake mode the set the temperature to pre-heat your Air Fryer at 360° F.

Once the Fryer has warmed up, put the cookies inside and leave to cook for 10 minutes. Take care when taking them out and allow to cook before enjoying.

Blackberry Crisp

Ready about in: 18 min | Servings: 1 | Normal

Ingredients

2 tablespoon lemon juice

1/3 cup powdered erythritol

¼ teaspoon xantham gum

2 cup blackberries

1 cup crunchy granola

Direction:

In a bowl, combine the lemon juice, erythritol, xantham gum, and blackberries. Transfer to a round baking dish about six inches in diameter and seal with aluminum foil.

Put the dish in the Air Fryer and leave to cook for 12 minutes at 350° F.

Take care when removing the dish from the fryer. Give the blackberries another stir and top with the granola.

Return the dish to the fryer and cook for an additional three minutes, this time at 320° F.

Serve once the granola has turned brown and enjoy.

Melts in Your Mouth Caramel Cheesecake

Ready about in: 40 min | Serves 8 | Difficult

Ingredients

1 Can Dulce de Leche

1 tablespoon Melted Chocolate

1 tablespoon Vanilla Essence

250 g Caster Sugar

4 Large Eggs

50 g Melted Butter

500 g Soft Cheese

6 Digestives, crumbled

Direction:

Lightly grease baking pan of Air Fryer with cooking spray. Mix and press crumbled digestives and melted butter on pan bottom. Spread dulce de leche.

In bowl, beat well soft cheese and sugar until fluffy. Stir in vanilla and egg. Pour over dulce de leche.

Cover pan with foil. For 15 minutes, cook on 390° F.

Cook for 10 minutes at 330° F. And then 15 minutes at 300° F.

Let it cool completely in Air Fryer. Refrigerate for at least 4 hours before slicing.

Serve and enjoy.

Butter Marshmallow Fluff Turnover

Ready about in: 35 min | Servings: 4 | Normal

Ingredients

4 sheets filo pastry, defrosted

4 tablespoon chunky peanut butter

4 teaspoon marshmallow fluff

2 ounce butter, melted

Pinch of sea salt

Direction:

Select bake mode the set the temperature to pre-heat the Air Fryer to 360° F.

Roll out the pastry sheets. Coat one with a light brushing of butter.

Lay a second pastry sheet on top of the first one. Brush once again with butter. Repeat until all 4 sheets have been used.

Slice the filo layers into four strips, measuring roughly 3 inches x 12 inches.

Spread one tablespoon of peanut butter and one teaspoon of marshmallow fluff on the underside of each pastry strip.

Take the tip of each sheet and fold it backwards over the filling, forming a triangle. Repeat this action in a zigzag manner until the filling is completely enclosed.

Seal the ends of each turnover with a light brushing of butter.

Put the turnovers in the Fryer basket and cook for 3 – 5 minutes, until they turn golden brown and puffy.

Sprinkle a little sea salt over each turnover before serving.

Orange Carrot Cake

Ready about in: 30 min | Servings: 8 | Normal

Ingredients

2 large carrots, peeled and grated

1 ¾ cup flour

¾ cup sugar

2 eggs

10 tablespoon olive oil

2 cups sugar

1 teaspoon mixed spice

2 tablespoon milk

4 tablespoon melted butter

1 small orange, rind and juice

Direction:

Set the Air Fryer to 360° F and allow to heat up for 10 minutes.

Place a baking sheet inside the tin.

Combine the flour, sugar, grated carrots, and mixed spice.

Pour the milk, beaten eggs, and olive oil into the middle of the batter and mix well.

Pour the mixture in the tin, transfer to the Fryer and cook for 5 minutes.

Lower the heat to 320° F and allow to cook for an additional 5 minutes.

In the meantime, prepare the frosting by combining the melted butter, orange juice, rind, and sugar until a smooth consistency is achieved.

Remove the cake from the Fryer, allow it to cool for several minutes and add the frosting on top.

Serve and Enjoy

English Lemon Tarts

Ready about in: 30 min | Servings: 4 | Normal

Ingredients

½ cup butter

½ lb. flour

2 tablespoon sugar

1 large lemon, juiced and zested

2 tablespoon lemon curd

Pinch of nutmeg

Direction:

In a large bowl, combine the butter, flour and sugar until a crumbly consistency is achieved.

Add in the lemon zest and juice, followed by a pinch of nutmeg. Continue to combine. If necessary, add a couple tablespoons of water to soften the dough.

Sprinkle the insides of a few small pastry tins with flour. Pour equal portions of the dough into each one and add sugar or lemon zest on top.

Select bake mode the set the temperature to pre-heat the Air Fryer to 360° F.

Place the lemon tarts inside the Fryer and allow to cook for 15 minutes.

When the timer reaches 0, then press the cancel button

Serve and Enjoy

Keto-Friendly Doughnut Recipe

Ready about in: 20 min | Serves 4 | Difficult

Ingredients

¼ cup coconut milk

¼ cup erythritol

¼ cup flaxseed meal

¾ cup almond flour

1 tablespoon cocoa powder

1 teaspoon vanilla extract

2 large eggs, beaten

3 tablespoons coconut oil

Direction:

Place all ingredients in a mixing bowl.

Mix until well-combined.

Scoop the dough into individual doughnut molds.

Select bake mode the set the temperature to preheat the Air Fryer for 5 minutes.

Cook for 20 minutes at 350° F.

Bake in batches if possible.

Serve and Enjoy

Maple Cinnamon Buns

Ready about in: 1 hr and 30 min | Serves 9 | Normal

Ingredients

¼ cup icing sugar

½ cup pecan nuts, toasted

¾ cup tablespoon unsweetened almond milk

1 ½ cup plain white flour, sifted

1 ½ tablespoon active yeast

1 cup wholegrain flour, sifted

1 tablespoon coconut oil, melted

1 tablespoon ground flaxseed

2 ripe bananas, sliced

2 teaspoons cinnamon powder

4 Medjool dates, pitted

4 tablespoons maple syrup

Direction:

Heat the ¾ cup almond milk to lukewarm and add the maple syrup and yeast. Allow the yeast to activate for 5 to 10 minutes.

Meanwhile, mix together flaxseed and 3 tablespoons of water to make the egg replacement. Allow flaxseed to soak for 2 minutes. Add the coconut oil.

Pour the flaxseed mixture to the yeast mixture.

In another bowl, combine the two types of flour and the 1 tablespoon cinnamon powder. Pour the yeast-flaxseed mixture and combine until dough forms.

Knead the dough on a floured surface for at least 10 minutes.

Place the kneaded dough in a greased bowl and cover with a kitchen towel. Leave in a warm and dark area for the bread to rise for 1 hour. While the dough is rising, make the filling by mixing together the pecans, banana slices, and dates. Add 1 tablespoon of cinnamon powder.

Preheat the Air Fryer to 390° F.

Roll the risen dough on a floured surface until it is thin. Spread the pecan mixture on to the dough.

Roll the dough and cut into nine slices.

Place inside a dish that will fit in the air fryer and cook for 30 minutes.

Once cooked, sprinkle with icing sugar.

Serve and Enjoy

Cherry Pie

Ready about in: 35 min | Servings: 8 | Easy

Ingredients

1 tablespoon milk

2 ready-made pie crusts

21 ounce cherry pie filling

1 egg yolk

Direction:

Select bake mode the set the temperature to pre-heat the Air Fryer to 310° F.

Coat the inside of a pie pan with a little oil or butter and lay one of the pie crusts inside. Use a fork to pierce a few holes in the pastry. Spread the pie filling evenly over the crust.

Slice the other crust into strips and place them on top of the pie filling to make the pie look more homemade.

Place in the Air Fryer and cook for 15 minutes.

When the timer reaches 0, then press the cancel button

Serve and Enjoy

Apple Pie

Ready about in: 25 min | Servings: 7 | Easy

Ingredients

2 large apples

½ cup flour

2 tablespoon unsalted butter

1 tablespoon sugar

½ teaspoons cinnamon

Direction:

Select bake mode the set the temperature to pre-heat the Air Fryer to 360° F

In a large bowl, combine the flour and butter. Pour in the sugar, continuing to mix.

Add in a few tablespoons of water and combine everything to create a smooth dough.

Grease the insides of a few small pastry tins with butter. Divide the dough between each tin and lay each portion flat inside.

Peel, core and dice up the apples. Put the diced apples on top of the pastry and top with a sprinkling of sugar and cinnamon.

Place the pastry tins in your Air Fryer and cook for 15 - 17 minutes. Serve with whipped cream or ice cream if desired.

Oriental Coconut Cake

Ready about in: 40 min | Serves 8 | Easy

Ingredients

1 cup gluten-free flour

2 eggs

1/2 cup flaked coconut

1-1/2 teaspoons baking powder

1/2 teaspoon baking soda

1/2 teaspoon xanthan gum

1/2 teaspoon salt

1/2 cup coconut milk

1/2 cup vegetable oil

1/2 teaspoon vanilla extract

1/4 cup chopped walnuts

3/4 cup white sugar

Direction:

In blender blend all wet Ingredients. Add dry ingredients and blend thoroughly.

Lightly grease baking pan of Air Fryer with cooking spray.

Pour in batter. Cover pan with foil.

For 30 minutes, cook on 330° F.

Let it rest for 10 minutes

Serve and enjoy.

Pound Cake with Fresh Apples

Ready about in: 60 min | Serves 6 | Normal

Ingredients

1 cup white sugar

1 teaspoon vanilla extract

1 medium Granny Smith apples - peeled, cored and chopped

1-1/2 eggs

1-1/2 cups all-purpose flour

1/2 teaspoon baking soda

1/2 teaspoon salt

1/4 teaspoon ground cinnamon

2/3 cup and 1 tablespoon chopped walnuts

3/4 cup vegetable oil

Direction:

In blender, blend all Ingredients except for apples and walnuts. Blend thoroughly. Fold in apples and walnuts.

Lightly grease baking pan of Air Fryer with cooking spray. Pour batter.

Cover pan with foil.

For 30 minutes, cook on preheated 330° F Air Fryer.

Remove foil and cook for another 20 minutes.

Let it stand for 10 minutes.

Serve and enjoy.

Raspberry-Coco Dessert

Ready about in: 20 min | Serves 12 | Easy

Ingredients

¼ cup coconut oil

1 cup coconut milk

1 cup raspberries, pulsed

1 teaspoon vanilla bean

1/3 cup erythritol powder

3 cups desiccated coconut

Direction:

Select bake mode the set the temperature to preheat the Air Fryer for 5 minutes.

Combine all ingredients in a mixing bowl.

Pour into a greased baking dish.

Bake in the Air Fryer for 20 minutes at 375° F.

When the timer reaches 0, then press the cancel button

Serve and Enjoy

Lava Cake in A Mug

Ready about in: 15 min | Serves 4 | Normal

Ingredients

¼ cup coconut oil, melted

¼ teaspoon vanilla powder

1 cup dark chocolate powder

1 tablespoon almond flour

2 tablespoons stevia powder

3 large eggs, beaten

Direction:

Select bake mode the set the temperature to preheat th Air Fryer for 5 minutes.

Combine all ingredients in a mixing bowl.

Grease ramekins with coconut oil and dust with chocolate powder.

Pour the batter into the ramekins and place in the Fryer basket.

Close and bake at 375° F for 15 minutes.

When the timer reaches 0, then press the cancel button

Serve and Enjoy!

Blueberry Pancakes

Ready about in: 20 min | Servings: 4 | Easy

Ingredients

½ teaspoon vanilla extract

2 tablespoon honey

½ cup blueberries

½ cup sugar

2 cups + 2 tablespoon flour

3 eggs, beaten

1 cup milk

1 teaspoon baking powder

Pinch of salt

Direction:

Select bake mode the set the temperature to pre-heat th Air Fryer to 390° F.

In a bowl, mix together all of the dry ingredients.

Pour in the wet ingredients and combine with a whisk, ensuring the mixture becomes smooth.

Roll each blueberry in some flour to lightly coat it before folding it into the mixture. This is to ensure they do not change the color of the batter.

Coat the inside of a baking dish with a little oil or butter.

Spoon several equal amounts of the batter onto the baking dish, spreading them into pancake-shapes and ensuring to space them out well. This may have to be completed in 2 batches.

Place the dish in the Fryer and bake for about 10 minutes.

Chocolate Brownies & Caramel Sauce

Ready about in: 45 minutes | Servings: 4 | Difficult

Ingredients

½ cup butter, plus more for greasing the pan

1 ¾ ounce unsweetened chocolate

1 cup sugar

2 medium eggs, beaten

1 cup flour

2 teaspoon vanilla

2 tablespoon water

2/3 cup milk

Direction:

In a saucepan over a medium heat, melt the butter and chocolate together.

Take the saucepan off the heat and stir in the sugar, eggs, flour, and vanilla, combining everything well.

Pre-heat your Air Fryer to 350° F.

Coat the inside of a baking dish with a little butter. Transfer the batter to the dish and place inside the fryer.

Bake for 15 minutes.

In the meantime, prepare the caramel sauce. In a small saucepan, slowly bring the water to a boil. Cook for around 3 minutes, until the mixture turns light brown.

Lower the heat and allow to cook for another two minutes. Gradually add in the rest of the butter. Take the saucepan off the heat and allow the caramel to cool.

When the brownies are ready, slice them into squares. Pour the caramel sauce on top and add on some sliced banana if desired before serving.

www.ingramcontent.com/pod-product-compliance
Lightning Source LLC
Chambersburg PA
CBHW070938080526
44589CB00013B/1561